Easter Joke Book For Kids

Kiddley Press

Introduction

We hope that you are ready to laugh, because this book is different from all the rest! This is not just your normal joke book, meant to be read all by itself. This book is an interactive game. It's meant to be played with family, friends, siblings or between two people that would like to prove who is funniest. Time to see who can keep their cool and a straight face, and who is the most humorous in the family!

The benefits this book will provide your kids:

- **Family bonding -** This is a fantastic way for parents to spend some quality time with their kids and do so laughing and making the funniest memories.

- **Build confidence -** Creating a safe environment for children to express themselves is key to building real self-confidence.

- **Vocabulary Improvement -** The jokes in this book are written with a mixture of easy and more intermediate words which will expand your child's vocabulary in a fun and easy going way, while sometimes giving them a bit of a challenge.

- **Improved comprehension -** These jokes will help to develop your child's interest to comprehend the meaning and context of the joke before they go and share it with their friends.

- **Builds a sense of humor -** Jokes help your child to develop a healthy sense of humor while getting their brains to work at the same time!

Rules of the Game

The Goal of the game is to make your opponent laugh!

- Two players per game

- Take turns and read one joke out loud at a time

- Face your opponent head on and stare at them!

- When someone laughs, the other person wins a point.

- A smile does not count as a point. The laugh must be audible - meaning you have to hear something for it to count!

The first person to get 10 points Wins!

What should you say to
a rabbit on Easter?

Hoppy Easter!

What bunny can't hop?

A chocolate one!

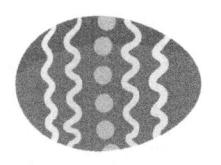

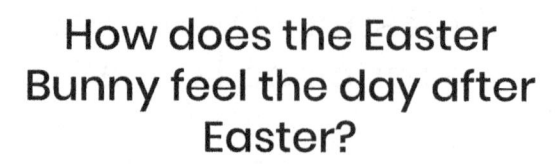

How does the Easter Bunny feel the day after Easter?

Eggs-hausted.

Why did the Easter Bunny cross the road?

Because the chicken stole his Easter eggs!

Where do Easter farts come from?

The Easter Bummy

Why did the bunny throw a temper tantrum?

Because he was hopping mad!

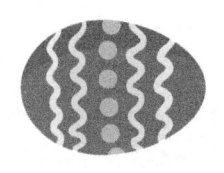

What do you get when you cross a bee and a rabbit?

A honey bunny.

HAPPY EASTER

Easter

Why did the Easter egg hide?

Because it was a little chicken.

What happens when you tell an egg a joke?

They crack up.

What's a bunny's favorite type of book?

One that has a hoppy ending.

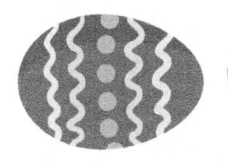

Which side of the Easter Bunny has the most fur?

The outside.

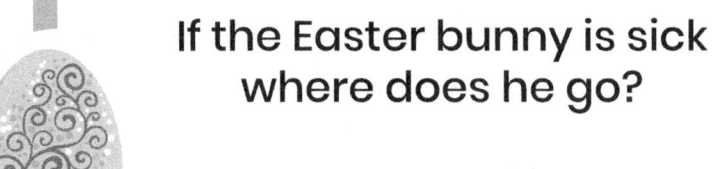

HAPPY EASTER

Easter

If the Easter bunny is sick where does he go?

The hoppital

Where do rabbits go after their Easter wedding?

On their bunnymoon!.

What is the Easter Bunny's favorite game?

Hopscotch!

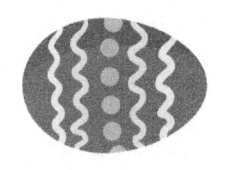

Why did the Easter Bunny throw the clock out the window?

He wanted to see time fly.

What do you call a rabbit that's brought up indoors?

An in-grown hare!

Why is rabbit farming a terrifying profession?

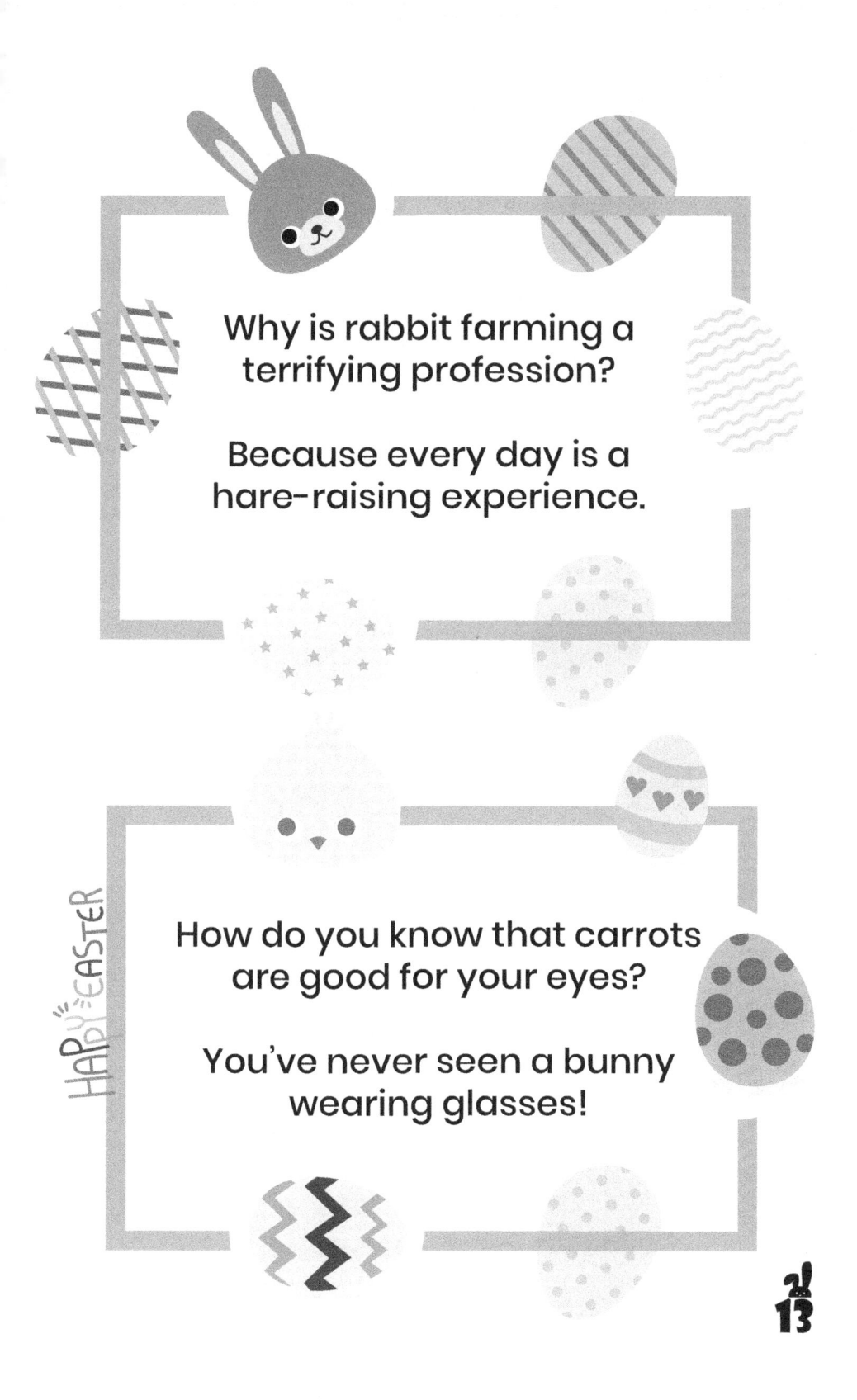

Because every day is a hare-raising experience.

How do you know that carrots are good for your eyes?

You've never seen a bunny wearing glasses!

Why don't you see dinosaurs on Easter?

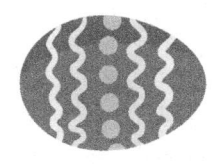

Because they're eggs-tinct.

HAPPY EASTER

Easter

I accidentally drank the water we used to color eggs for Easter.

I think I might have dyed a little inside.

Where did the Easter bunny go when there was a fire in the building?

To the emergency eggs-it

How do you turn light chocolate into dark chocolate?

You turn off the lights

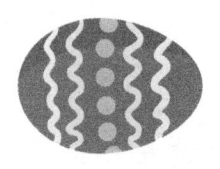

Which button can't you un-button after Easter lunch?

Your belly button!

Easter

Why are eggs so salty?

Because they didn't get to be chickens

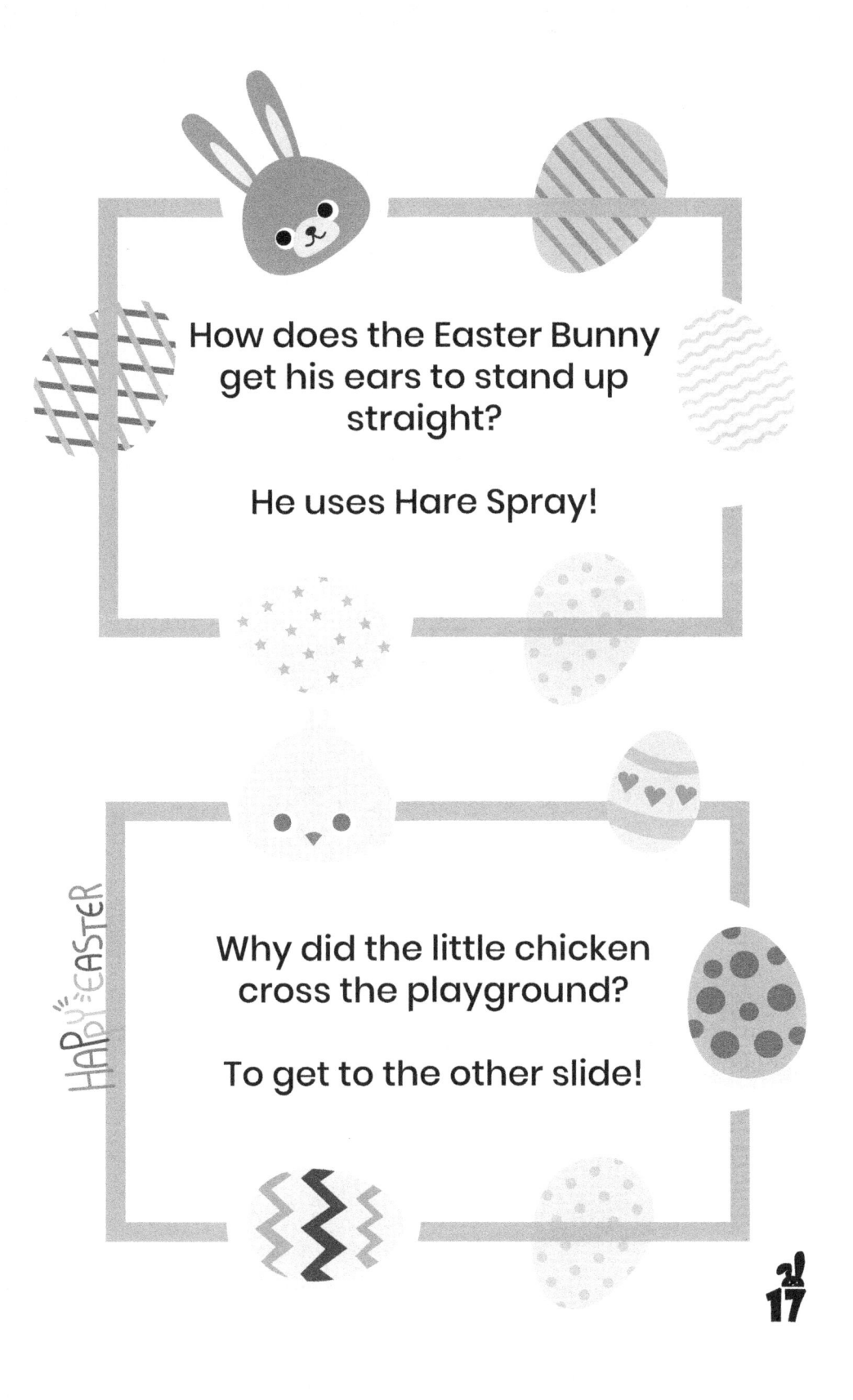

How does the Easter Bunny get his ears to stand up straight?

He uses Hare Spray!

Why did the little chicken cross the playground?

To get to the other slide!

Where do Eskimos keep their Easter eggs?

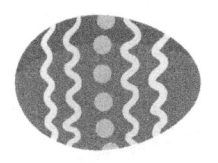

Inside an egg-loo!

Why can't eggs keep secrets?

Because they tend to crack under pressure

Who tells the best egg jokes?

The comedy-hens!

What kind of music does the Easter Bunny like?

Hip-hop!

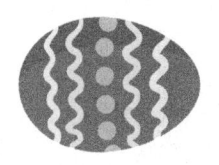

What would you call a frightened egg?

Terri-fried!

Easter

What day do Easter eggs hate the most?

Fry-day.

What is an Easter egg from outer space called?

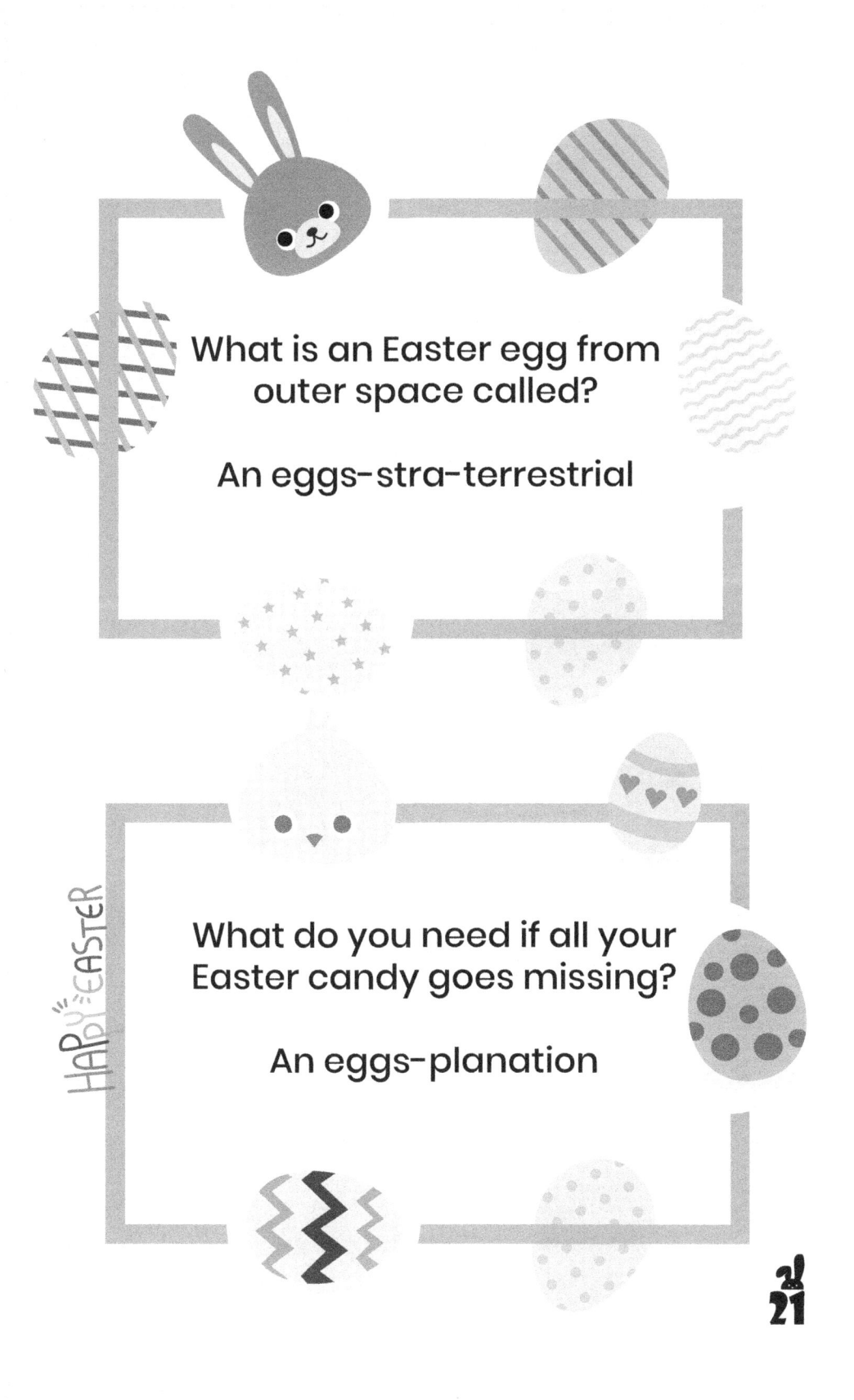

An eggs-stra-terrestrial

What do you need if all your Easter candy goes missing?

An eggs-planation

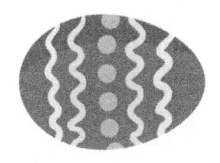

How do you catch the Easter Bunny?

Hide in the bushes and make a noise like a carrot!

Which dance is the Easter Bunny's favorite?

The bunny hop!

What should you call a rabbit that tells jokes?

A funny bunny

Did you hear about the man who had a house infested with Easter eggs?

He had to call the eggs-terminator!

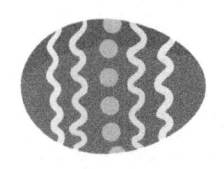

Do you know where the Easter Bunny gets his eggs from?

The Egg-plant!

What kind of fruit loves chocolate?

A coco-nut.

Do you know what you call a rabbit with fleas?

Bugs Bunny!

What will happen to the Easter Bunny if he misbehaves at school?

He'll get eggs-pelled!

If you pour hot water down a rabbit hole, what do you get?

Hot cross bunnies!

HAPPY EASTER

Easter

What happens if you fall in love on Easter?

You will live hoppily ever after.

Why did the old bunny bring toilet paper to the Easter Party?

Because he's a party pooper!

Do you know how Easter ends?

With an "R"!

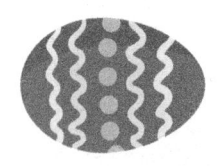

How does the Easter Bunny keep himself healthy?

He does lots of eggs-ercise

Happy Easter

Easter

How many Easter eggs can you put into an empty basket?

One - after that it's not empty anymore!

Where did the Easter Bunny study medicine?

Johns Hopkins

Why don't Easter eggs want to go out at night?

They might get beat up!

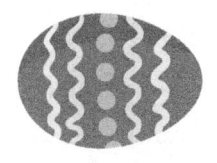

Why did the Easter Bunny wear a hat?

Because he had a bad hare-day.

HAPPY EASTER

Easter

What is the Easter Bunny's favorite place to eat breakfast?

IHOP

What does the Easter Bunny use to dry itself?

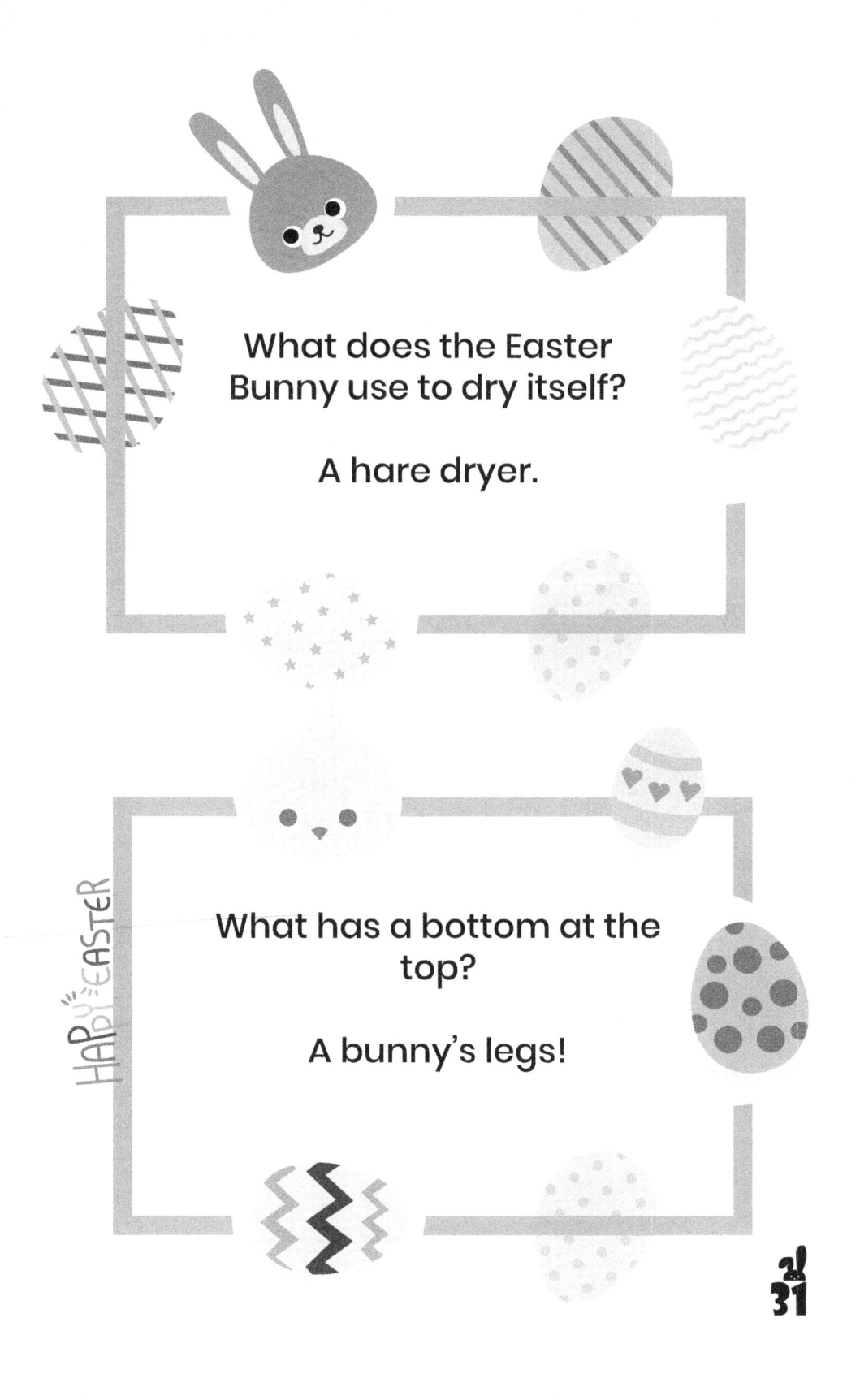

A hare dryer.

What has a bottom at the top?

A bunny's legs!

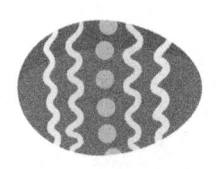

What do you call a naughty Easter egg?

A practical yolker

HAPPY EASTER

Easter

What kind of jokes does the Easter Bunny make in the shower?

Clean Jokes!

What do you call a group rabbits jumping backwards?

A receding hare-line!

Where does the Easter Bunny go when he needs a new tail?

To a re-tail store!

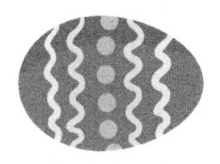

How are you able to tell which rabbits are oldest in a group?

Just look for the gray hares.

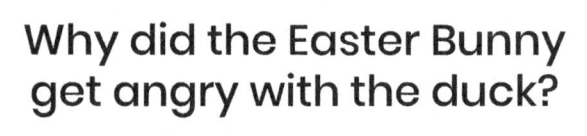

Why did the Easter Bunny get angry with the duck?

Because he kept quacking the eggs!

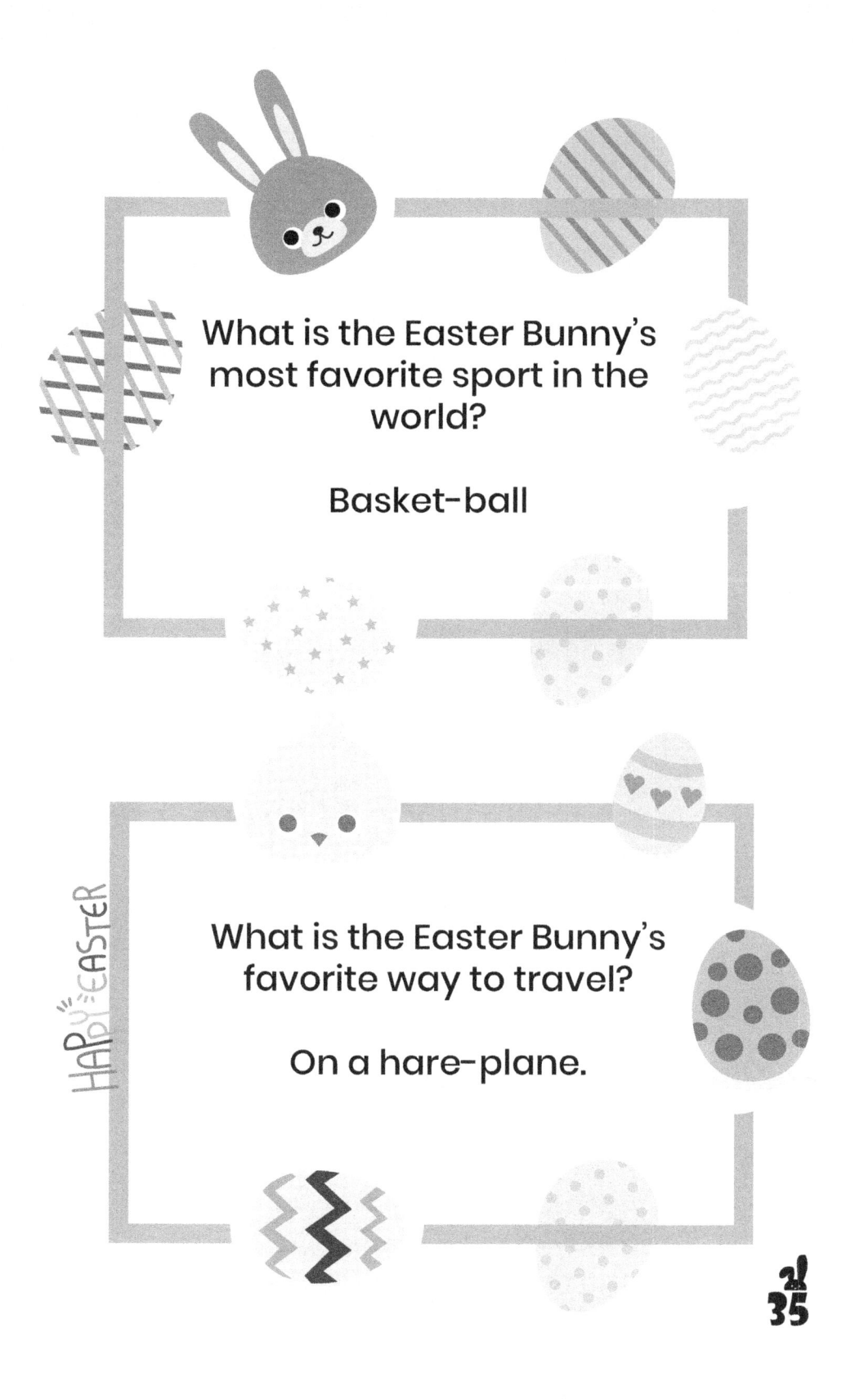

What is the Easter Bunny's most favorite sport in the world?

Basket-ball

What is the Easter Bunny's favorite way to travel?

On a hare-plane.

Therapist: How have you been feeling lately?

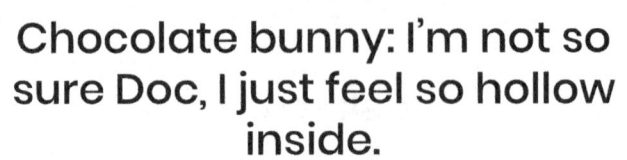

Chocolate bunny: I'm not so sure Doc, I just feel so hollow inside.

What did the rabbit say to the duck?

You quack me up!

What did the Easter bunny say to the carrot?

It's been nice gnawing you.

What did one egg say to the other?

Got any good yolks to tell me?

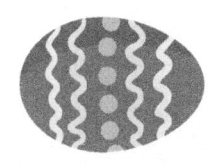

What did the bunny say about the Easter party?

That It was eggs-cellent.

HAPPY EASTER

Easter

What do you get when you cross a rabbit with a shellfish?

An oyster bunny!

What's the Easter Bunny's favorite type of jewelry?

14 - carrot gold earrings

How do you speed up your Easter present shopping?

Use the eggs-press lane!

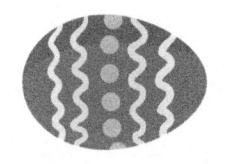

Why did the Easter egg fail at school?

Because he didn't study for his eggs-ams.

What is an egg's favorite kind of coffee?

An eggspresso of course!

What type of candy can never be on time?

choco-LATE.

Why did the Easter bunny put candy under his pillow?

Because he wanted some sweet dreams!

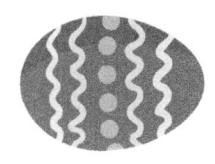

Why did the chicken go to jail?

Because he used fowl language!

Why should you be careful what you say around egg whites?

Because they can't take a yolk!

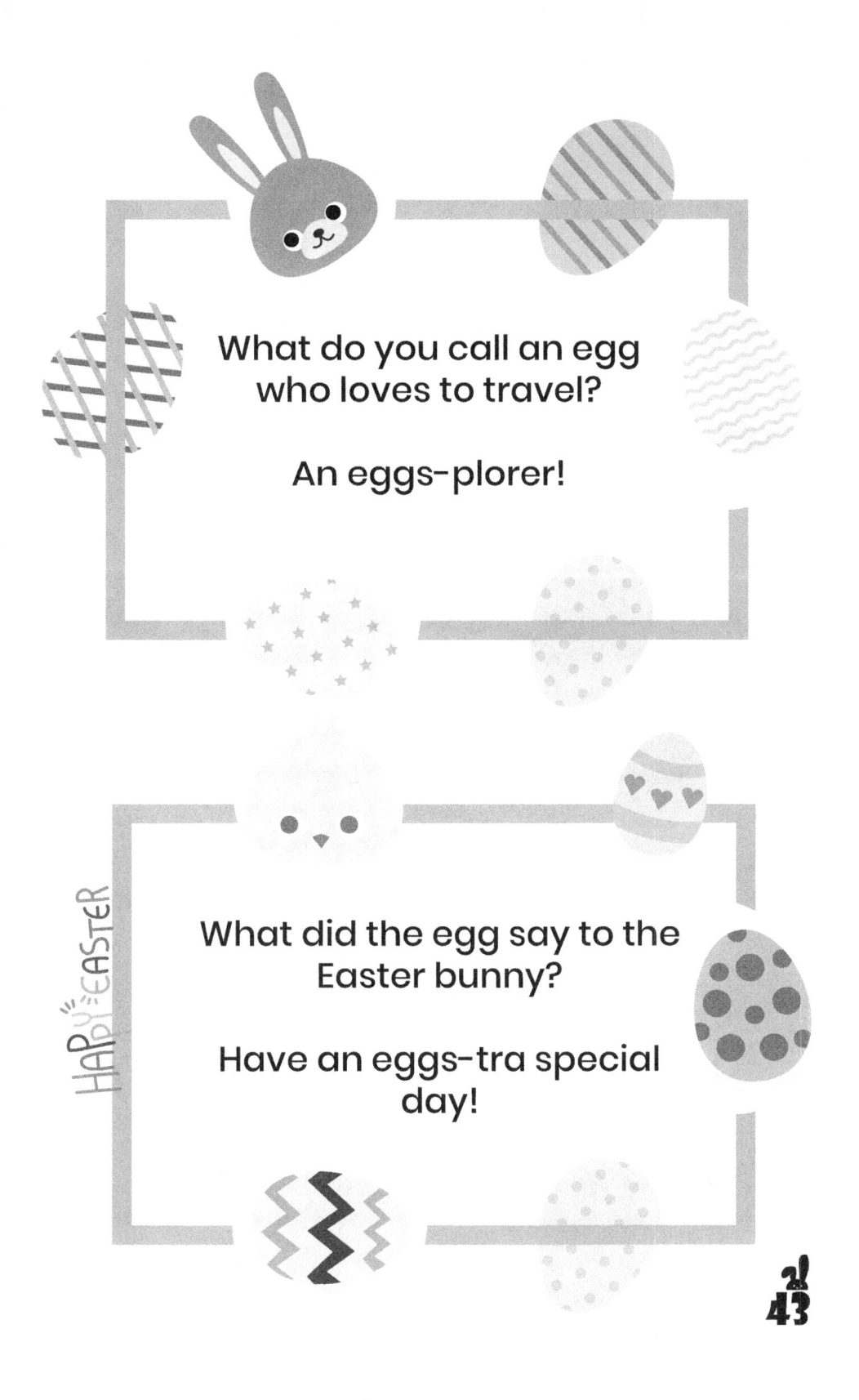

What do you call an egg who loves to travel?

An eggs-plorer!

What did the egg say to the Easter bunny?

Have an eggs-tra special day!

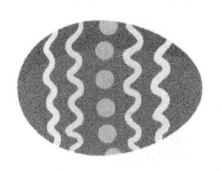

What did the egg do when it saw the frying pan?

It scrambled!

Where is the best place to learn about Easter eggs?

In the hen-cyclopedia!

When is the best time to eat your Easter eggs?

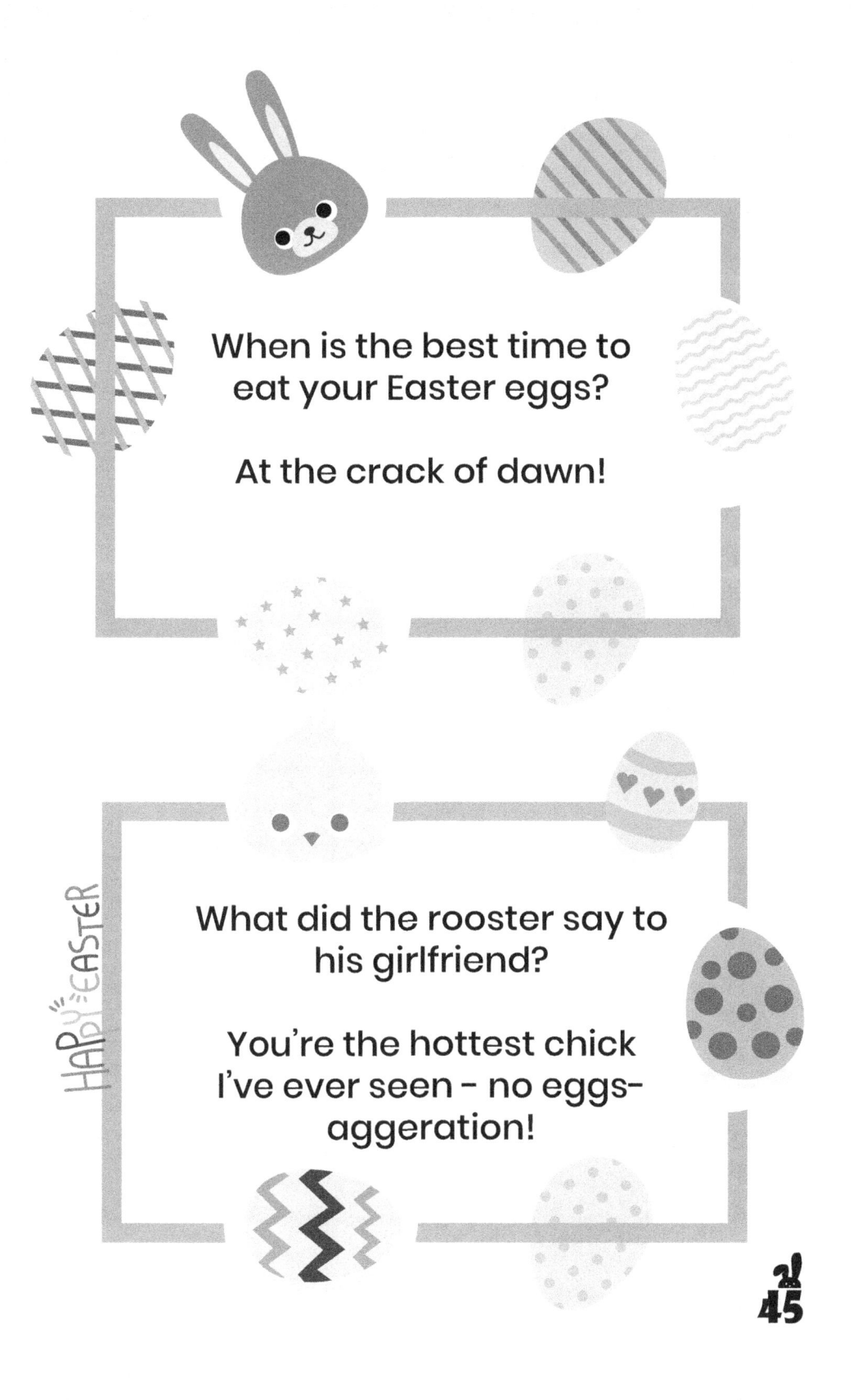

At the crack of dawn!

What did the rooster say to his girlfriend?

You're the hottest chick I've ever seen - no eggs-aggeration!

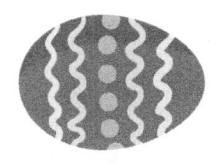

Why did the orange lose the race?

It ran out of juice!

How did the Easter egg find out it was sick?

It had an eggs-amination

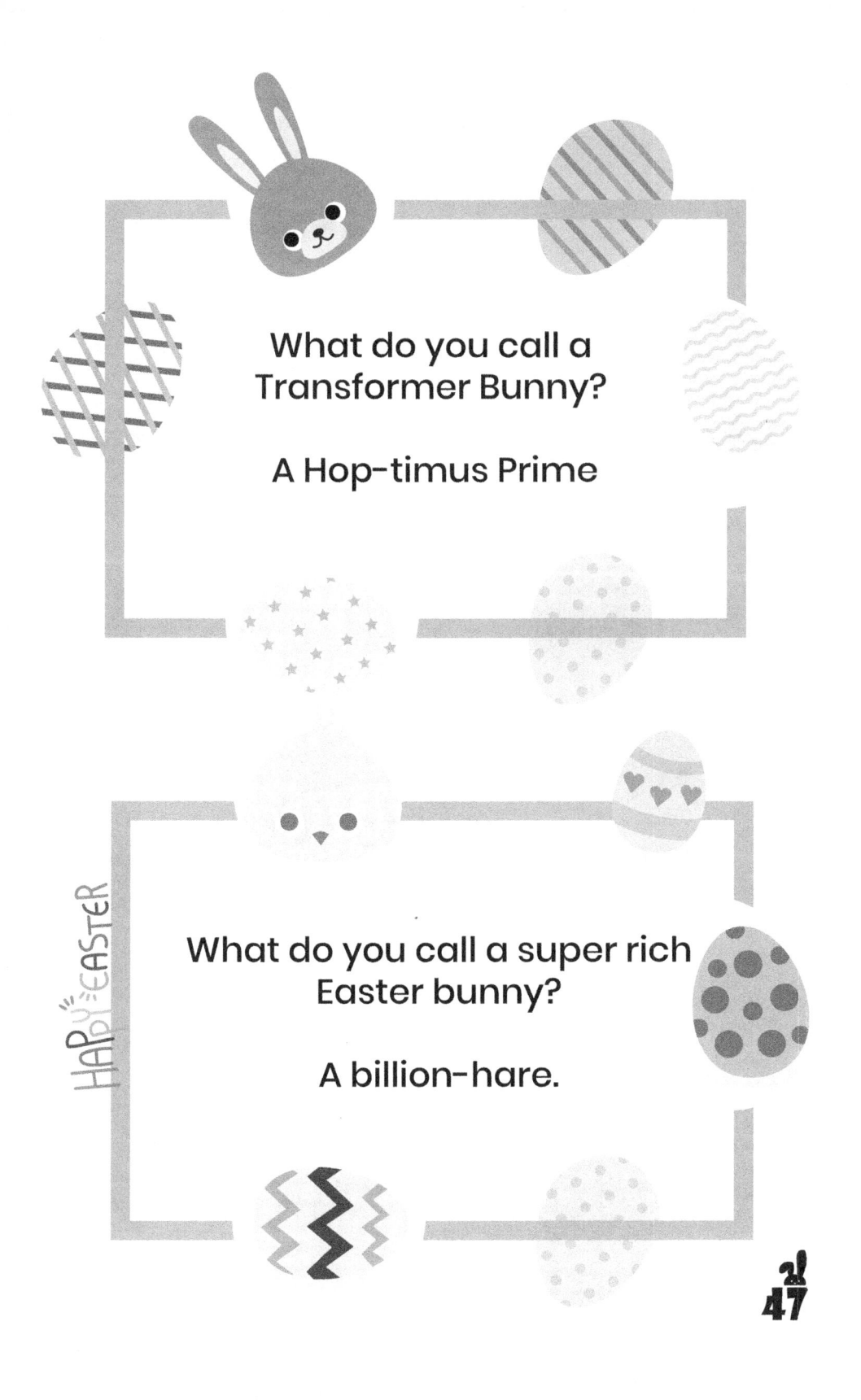

What do you call a
Transformer Bunny?

A Hop-timus Prime

What do you call a super rich
Easter bunny?

A billion-hare.

What does an evil hen lay?

Deviled eggs!

Why was the Easter bunny so tired in April?

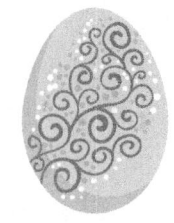

Because he just finished a March.

What do you call an egg when it meditates?

An ommmmmmlet.

How would you send a letter to the Easter Bunny?

Via hare mail.

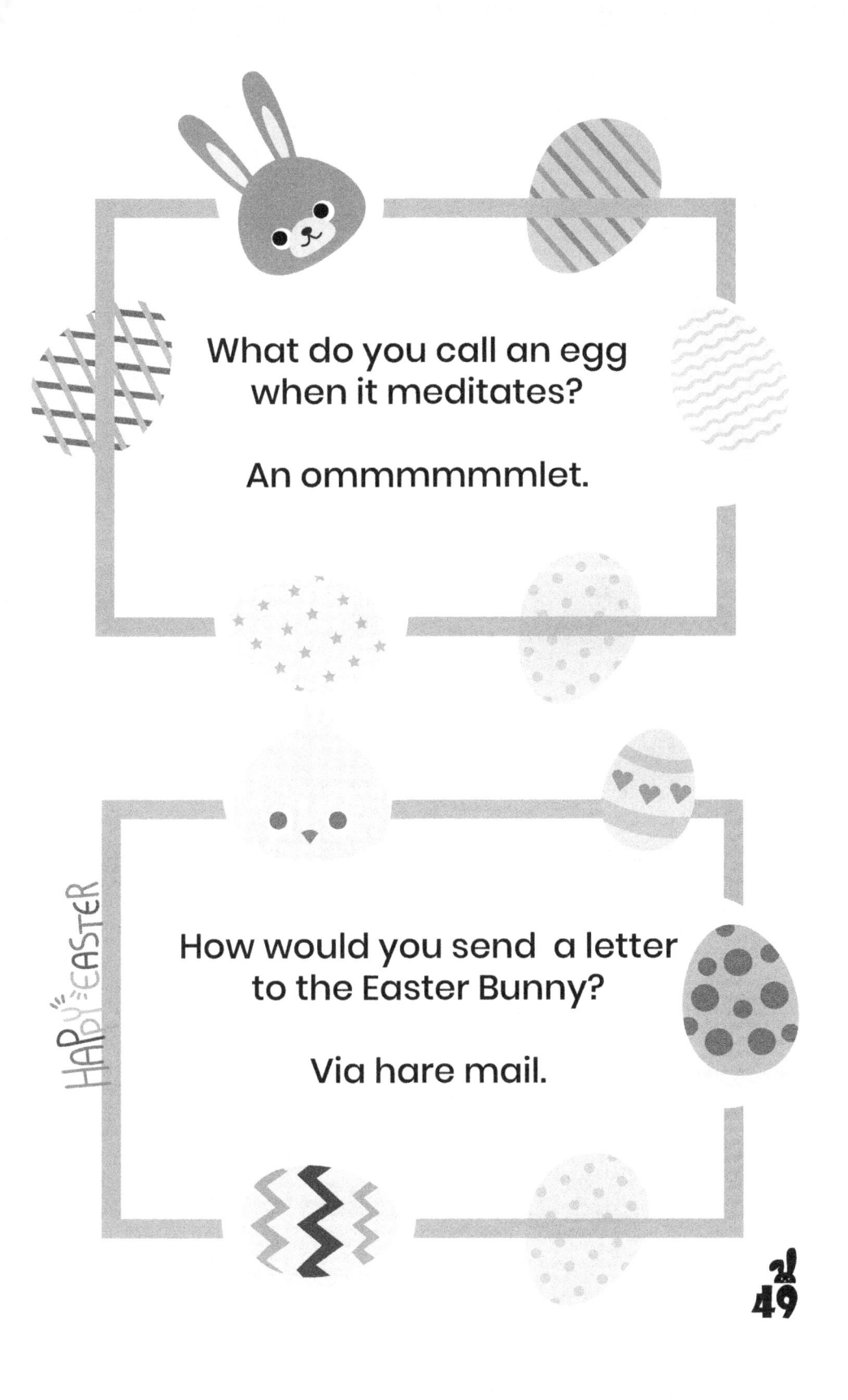

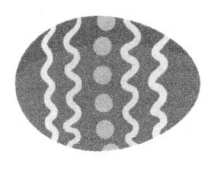

How do Easter bunnies keep fit?

Hare-robics.

What's the difference between a healthy bunny and a clown bunny?

One is a fit bunny and the other is a bit funny.

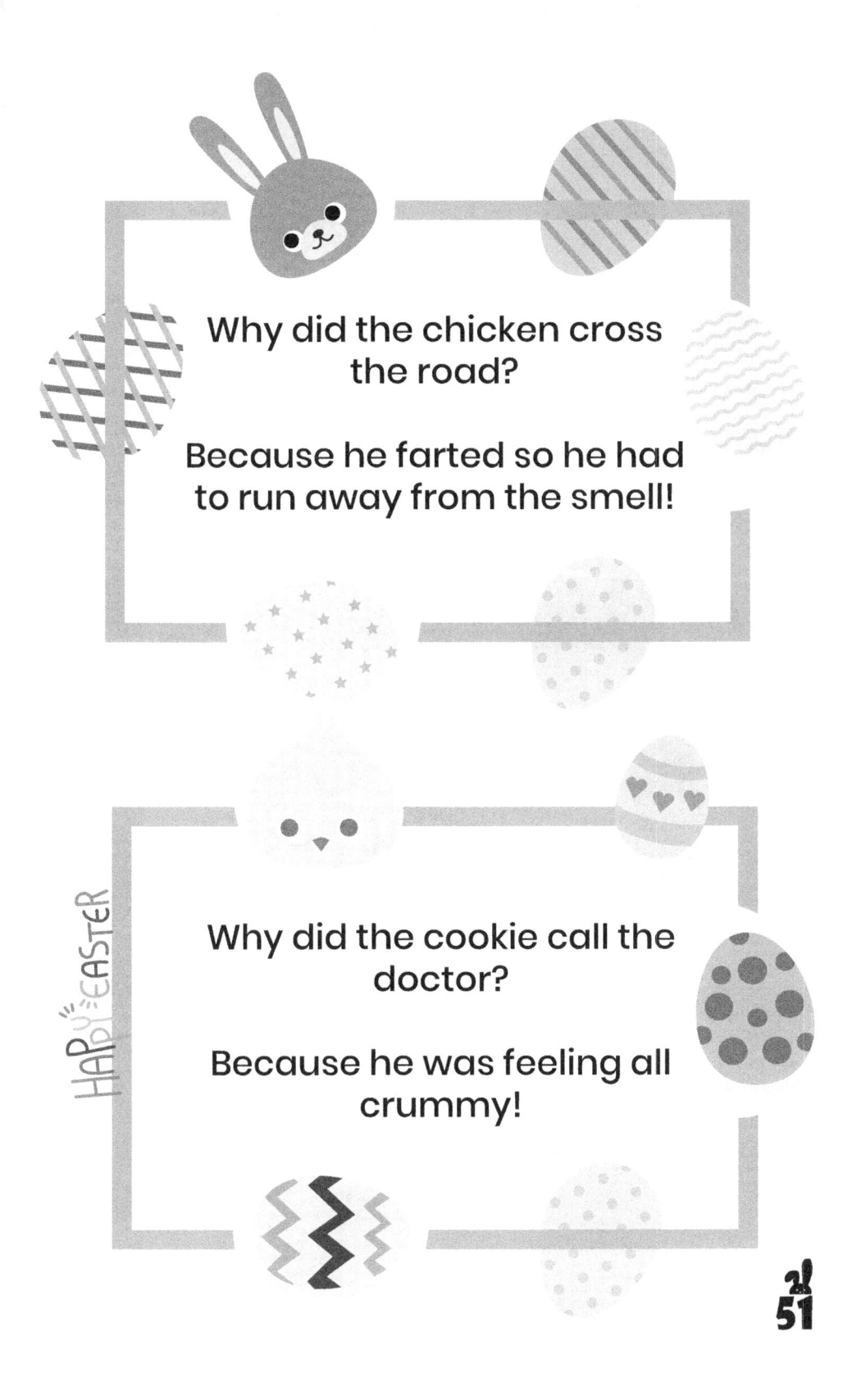

Why did the chicken cross the road?

Because he farted so he had to run away from the smell!

Why did the cookie call the doctor?

Because he was feeling all crummy!

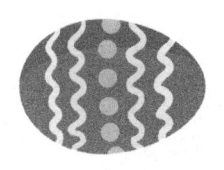

Why did the bunny leave his job?

He wanted a bigger celery.

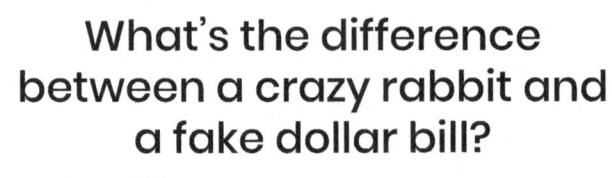

HAPPY EASTER

Easter

What's the difference between a crazy rabbit and a fake dollar bill?

One is a mad bunny and the other is bad money.

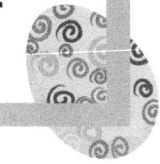

Why did the Easter bunny eat his homework?

Because his teacher said it was a piece of cake!

What do Easter bunny's say before they eat?

Lettuce pray.

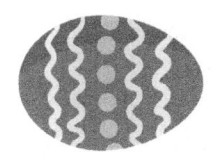

What do you call a cold doggie sitting on a rabbit?

A chili dog on a bun!

HAPPY EASTER

Easter

Why did the Easter bunny build himself a new house?

He was fed up with the hole thing!

Where do Easter bunnies learn how to fly?

In the hare force.

How do you make holy water?

Boil the hell out of it.

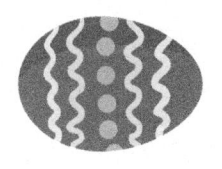

What country did candy first come from?

Sweeten

What do you call a bear that has no teeth?

A gummy bear!

What do you call a train that's filled with bubblegum?

A chew - chew train.

What is the Easter bunny's favorite type of candy?

Lolli-hops.

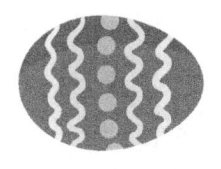

What happened to the bunny who only ate Skittles?

He farted rainbows.

HAPPY EASTER

Easter

What do kittens like to eat on easter?

Mice Cream

What do you call the Easter bunny with bananas in his ears?

Anything you want, he can't hear you

What's orange and sounds like a parrot?

A carrot

What do eggs love to do for fun with friends?

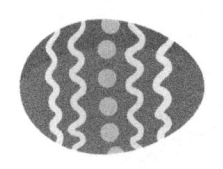

Kara-yolk-kee

What do you call a chocolate bunny?

Delicious!

Why didn't the egg cross the road?

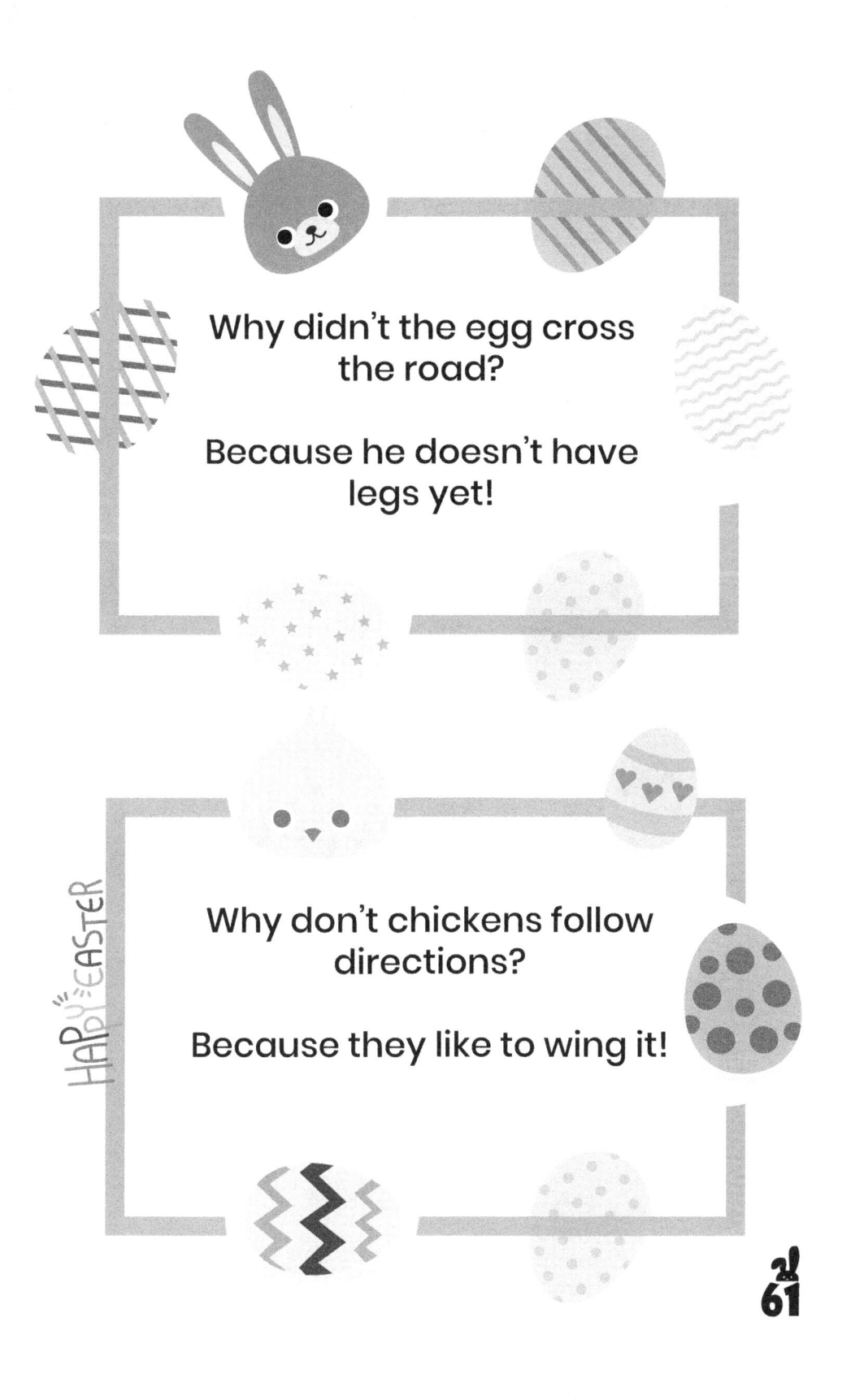

Because he doesn't have legs yet!

Why don't chickens follow directions?

Because they like to wing it!

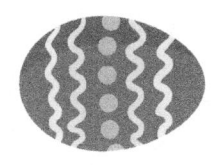

What did the mother egg say to the baby egg?

You are "Egg-stra special"!

HAPPY EASTER

Easter

What is yellow, has very long ears, and grows on trees?

The Easter Bunana!

What do you get when you cross the Easter Bunny with some Chinese food?

Hop-suey!

How is the Easter Bunny like Michael Jordan?

They're both famous for stuffing baskets!

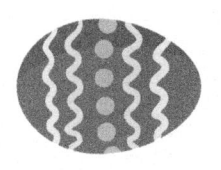

Why was the father Easter egg always so strict?

He was hard-boiled.

Why did the Creme egg go to the dentist?

Because he lost his filling!

What do you call Chewbacca when he has chocolate stuck in his hair?

Chocolate Chip Wookiee.

What do you call a hen that counts her eggs?

A mathemachicken

HAPPY EASTER

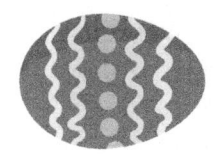

Why does a duck have feathers?

To cover his butt quack

Easter

Why Did the egg start speaking to strangers?

Because he needed to get out of his shell.

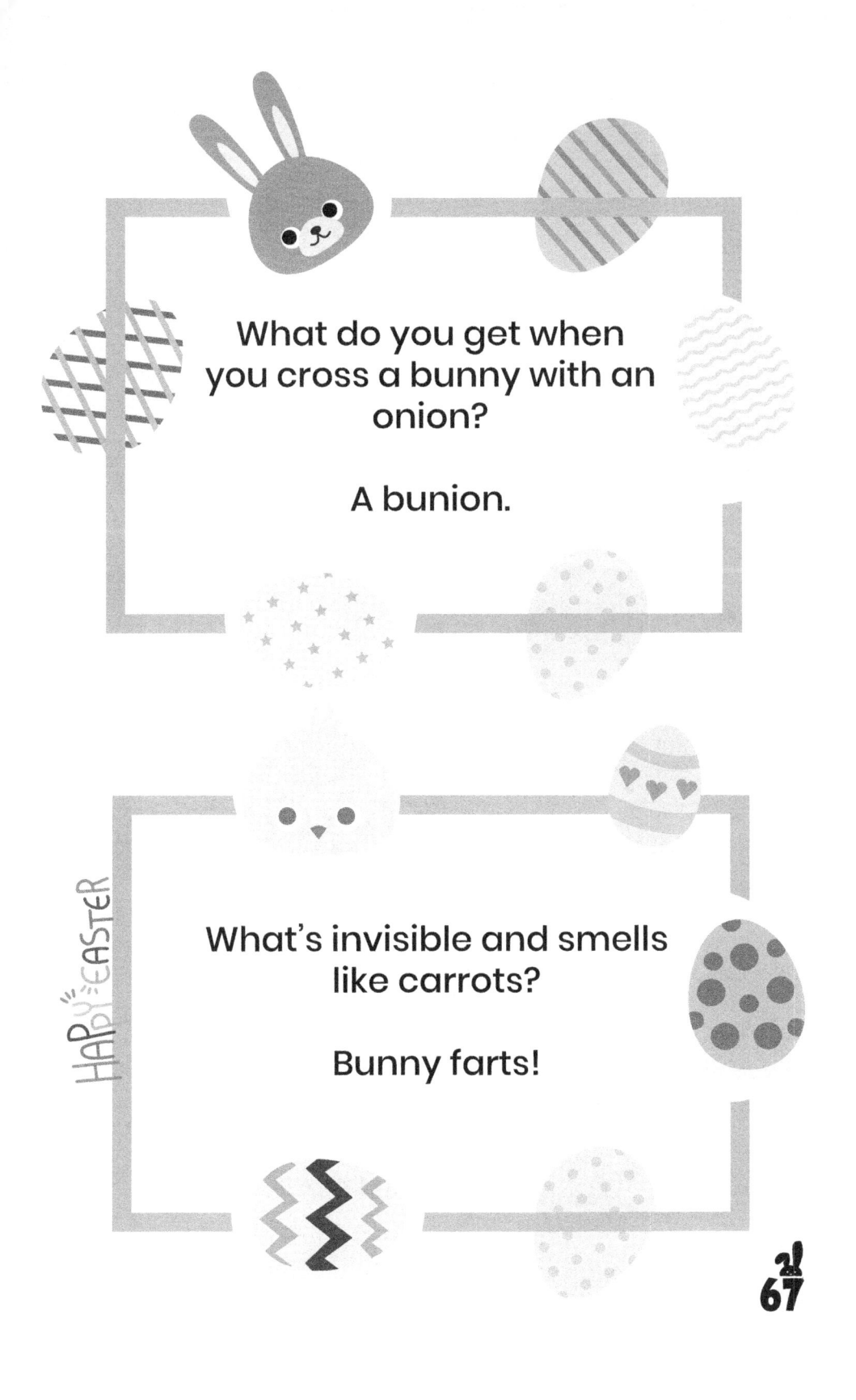

What do you get when you cross a bunny with an onion?

A bunion.

What's invisible and smells like carrots?

Bunny farts!

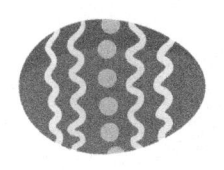

Why can't you sniff out Easter Eggs?

No bunny nose

HAPPY EASTER

Easter

How do you make a Chocolate omelet?

With Easter eggs.

Why did the Easter bunny hop around his bed?

To catch up on sleep.

Why can't the speckled egg play hide and seek?

Because he's always spotted

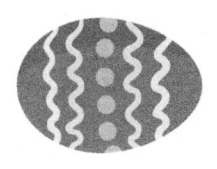

What does the Easter bunny say when he burps?

Eggs-cuse me!

What do you do if you see a bunny laying little brown eggs?

Don't eat them! It's not chocolate.

What do you call the Easter bunny if he eats all the carrots you left for him?

A pig!

What do you call a bunny with a cold?

A runny bunny

What do you call a sheep covered in chocolate?

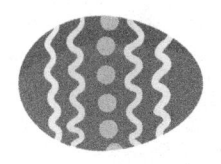

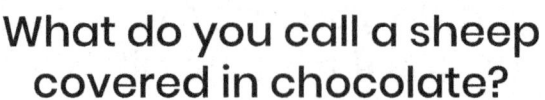

A chocolate baaa.

HAPPY EASTER

Easter

What did the grey bunny say to the blue bunny?

Cheer up!

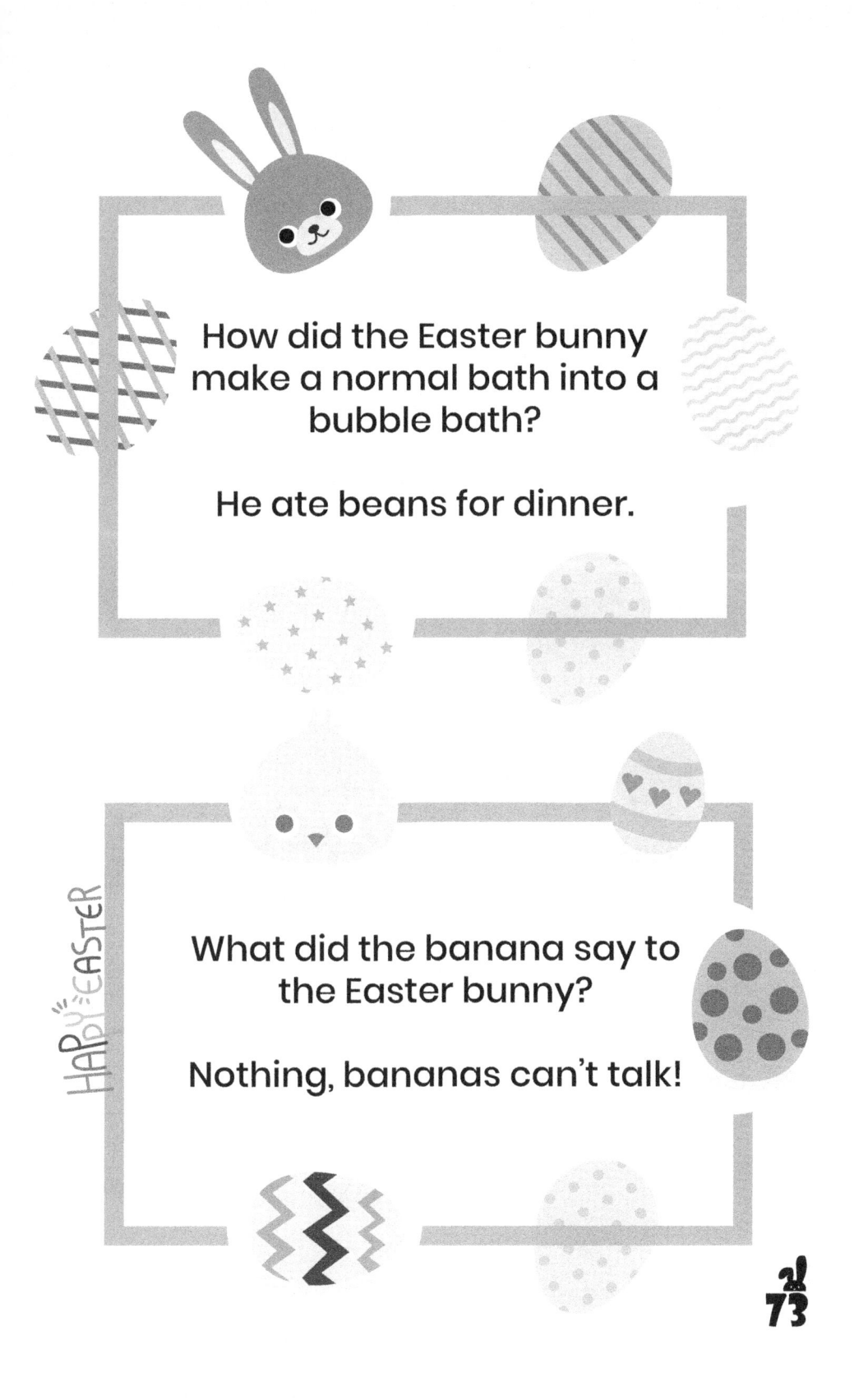

How did the Easter bunny make a normal bath into a bubble bath?

He ate beans for dinner.

What did the banana say to the Easter bunny?

Nothing, bananas can't talk!

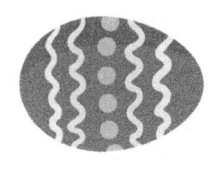

What do you call a bunny with a large brain?

An egghead.

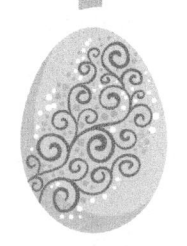

What happens if you eat too many Easter eggs?

An Eggs-plosion!

What animal can jump higher than a tree?

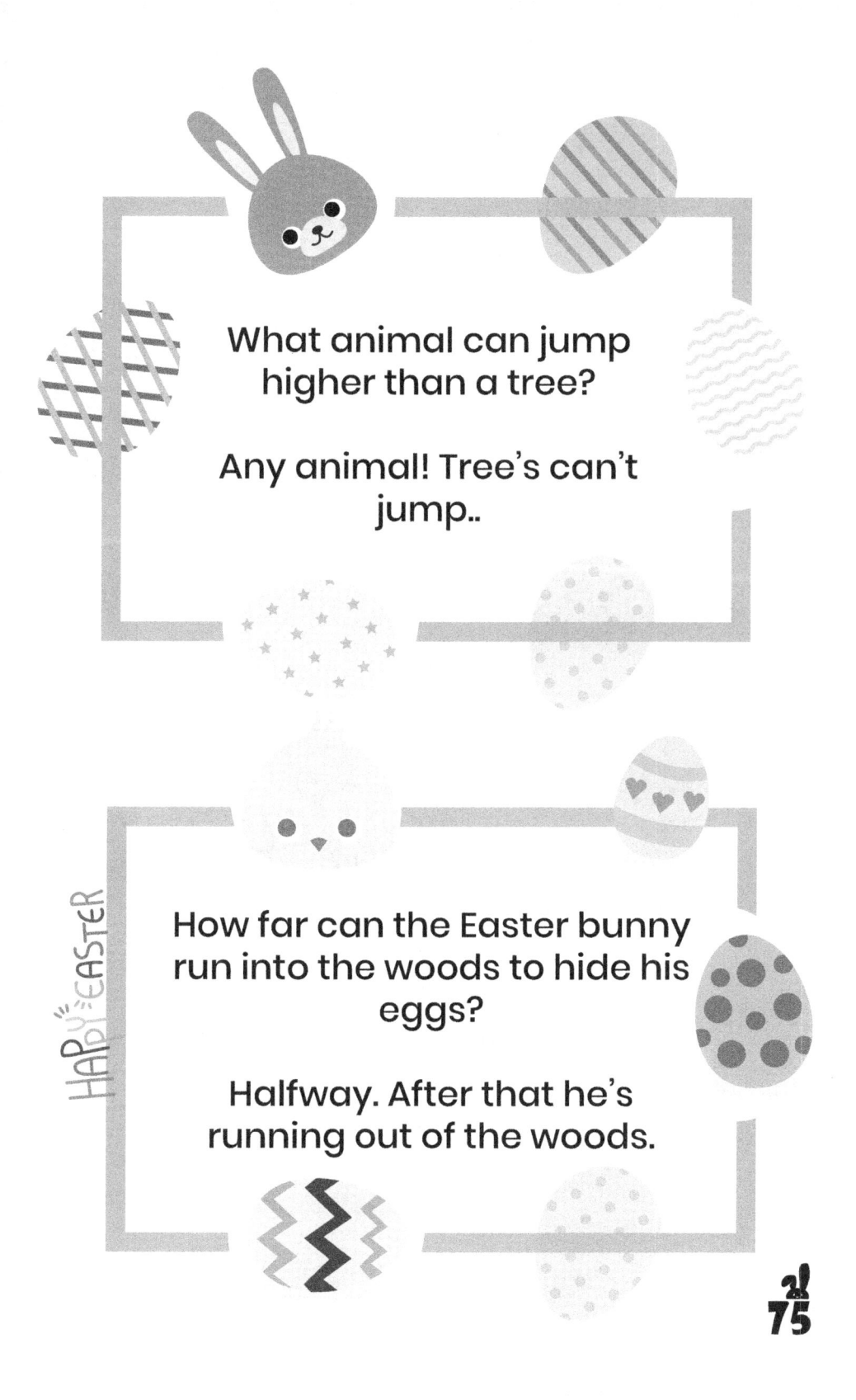

Any animal! Tree's can't jump..

How far can the Easter bunny run into the woods to hide his eggs?

Halfway. After that he's running out of the woods.

Why did the chicken feel left out?

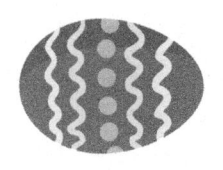

Because the eggs had an inside yolk

HAPPY EASTER

Easter

What did the cake say when no-one wanted to eat him on Easter?

I feel deserted

The End.... Almost!

We hope you liked this book and that it got plenty of smiles and chuckles out of your little ones this Easter!

Here's something that is not a joke, reviews - they can make or break an author's career.

As a small independent author with a tiny budget, I rely on readers, like you, to leave reviews on Amazon.

Even if it's just a sentence or two.

So if you enjoyed this book please leave me a brief review.

I very much appreciate every review that I receive and it truly makes a difference!

Thank you for purchasing this book and reading all the way to the end.

Hoppy Easter!

Made in the USA
Monee, IL
08 April 2022